# Cheers!

## Entertaining
## After-Dinner Stories
## from the Famous

*Collected by*
# PHYLLIS SHINDLER

PIATKUS

First published in 1995 by
Judy Piatkus (Publishers) Ltd of
5 Windmill Street, London W1P 1HF

**The moral right of the author has been asserted**

*A catalogue record for this book is available from the
British Library*

ISBN  0-7499-1561-7 (hbk)
       0-7499-1527-7 (pbk)

Illustrations by Ellis Nadler

Typeset in 11/13pt Linotron Palatino by
Phoenix Photosetting, Chatham, Kent
Printed and bound in Great Britain by
Mackays of Chatham PLC, Chatham, Kent

St. Bartholomew's Hospital has built a new laboratory specifically for cancer research. I am happy to devote the royalties from this, my fifth book, to help provide urgently needed medical equipment for the laboratory.

My thanks to those who have taken the time and trouble to provide stories and anecdotes.

Donations have been sent by others, including His Royal Highness The Prince of Wales, and I am deeply appreciative of their support.

My gratitude to those who have purchased the book, together with the hope that it will give pleasure to the reader.

Phyllis Shindler

# Contributors

Foreword by Professor James Malpas, Director, Children's Cancer Unit, St. Bartholomew's Hospital 9

Maureen Lipman  *67*

Bryan Magee  *68*

Lady Olga Maitland  *69*

Christopher Martin-
Jenkins  *70*

Leo McKern  *72*

Sir David McNee  *73*

The Rt. Hon. David
Mellor  *75*

Dr. Patrick Moore  *76*

Michael Noakes  *77*

Denis Norden  *78*

John Julius Norwich  *79*

The Rt. Hon. Lord
Parkinson  *80*

Richard Pasco  *82*

Bill Pertwee  *83*

Frederic Raphael  *84*

H.E. Moshe Raviv,
Ambassador of Israel  *85*

Lord Renton  *86*

Sir Julian Ridsdale  *87*

Lord Rix  *88*

Willy Russell  *89*

Sir Peter Saunders  *90*

David Shepherd  *91*

Lord Stafford  *93*

Lord Stevens of
Ludgate  *94*

Alastair Stewart  *95*

Chris Tarrant  *96*

Leslie Thomas  *98*

Bill Tidy  *99*

Alan Titchmarsh  *100*

Lord Vestey  *101*

Terry Waite  *103*

Ian Wallace  *104*

Keith Waterhouse  *106*

Katharine Whitehorn  *107*

The Rt. Hon. Viscount
Whitelaw  *108*

Kenneth Wolstenholme  *109*

# Foreword
## by Professor James Malpas, D.Phil., F.R.C.P., D.R.C.R., F.R.C.R., F.F.P.M. Director, Children's Cancer Unit, St. Bartholomew's Hospital

It is a great pleasure to write this foreword for Phyllis Shindler's latest collection of after-dinner stories.

This collection will, I hope, not only raise a smile on your face but I am sure it will do the same for the devoted children's cancer research team at St. Bartholomew's Hospital, who receive the royalties.

To everyone who has contributed to the project, may I say how grateful we are and assure all those who buy this book that their money is well spent.

# The Rt. Hon. Marquess of Aberdeen

Member, International Association of Art Critics.
Bach Choir

During the last war a compartment of a Hungarian train contained four people: in one corner, a beautiful young girl; opposite her, a grand and stately old lady; in the other two corners, a Hungarian officer and a German officer.

The train entered a tunnel and there were no lights in the compartment. In the darkness there was the sound of a lascivious kiss, followed by a hard slap.

When the train emerged from the tunnel, the German had a black eye.

The old lady thought, 'What a good girl resisting the advances of that German.'

The young girl thought, 'That handsome German – I've had my eye on him; silly of him to kiss the old lady by mistake.'

The German thought, 'Blast that Hungarian – he goes for a kiss and I get hit for it.'

The Hungarian thought, 'I'm a clever fellow; I kiss the back of my hand, hit a German, and get away with it!'

\*　　　\*　　　\*

A knight set off for the Crusades, having given the key of his wife's chastity belt to his best friend for safekeeping.

As he trotted towards the Dover ferry, he heard the sound of a galloping horse coming up behind him. In a flurry of dust, the best friend reined in his horse and held up something shiny.

'Wrong key!' he said.

# Joan Aitken
Writer of Historical, Mystery and Children's Books

Here is a family story which we all found quite funny. It relates to my stepfather Martin Armstrong, a well-known writer of the 1930s who died some years ago in his nineties.

In his last few years he became very forgetful indeed, and one member of the family always had to be with him to keep an eye on him. One day, when I was in charge, I drove him to Chichester, our nearest large town, to get his hair cut. I left him at Emil's, his usual hairdressing establishment, and then had to park the car some distance away as the centre of Chichester, even then, was very congested.

When I left him at the barber's, I said to the girl at the cash desk: 'When this old gentleman has had his hair cut, *please* don't let him go out in the street. Tell him I'll be back for him in five minutes.' She promised to do so, and I drove away at top speed, parked in a car park and came racing back.

When I returned to Emil's, the girl said: 'There you are, I've kept your old gentleman for you.' But, alas, she had kept the wrong old gentleman (who seemed very indignant) and Martin had escaped into the street! It took me twenty minutes to track him down.

# Peter Alliss
Golfer, Television Commentator, Author

Ben Hogan, arguably the greatest striker of a golf ball the world has ever seen, was not renowned for his verbosity. In fact, his cold, clinical eye and lack of ebullience were legendary and the stories of his cutting remarks, bordering on the unkind, are well known – although many people, including myself, feel that on occasion he was hard done by.

One classic example comes to mind. There was a good amateur player called R.H. (Dick) Sykes who, after a fine amateur record in American golf, turned professional. He wasn't having a particularly good time, so he contacted Ben Hogan (who, throughout his golfing life, was almost unapproachable) and managed to arrange a game with the great man.

The day dawned. Sykes, a little nervous, and Hogan, dressed as usual in light and dark grey, a permanent cigarette in the corner of his mouth, set off towards the first tee. En route Sykes remarked, 'I'm so delighted that you've given up your time to see me. I don't know what's wrong; if it weren't for my short game I'd be in a terrible mess – it's the only thing that's keeping me going.'

They struck off from the first tee and hardly a word was said until the eighteen holes were completed. On the way back to the locker room, Sykes turned to Hogan and said, in slight fear and trepidation, 'Well, Mr Hogan, did you spot anything?' Hogan gave him one of his steely looks and said, 'Your short game isn't much good either.'

End of story!

# Lord Archer of Weston-Super-Mare
Politician, Author

The Chairman of a Conservative Constituency visited his MP when he was ill in hospital. It was well known that the Executive Committee rather hoped Sir Peter would stand down at the next Election, which he may have gathered when the Chairman told him:

'I put forward a resolution at our last meeting, hoping that the Member would have a quick and speedy recovery.'

'Oh, how kind.'

'This was passed,' said the Chairman, 'by eleven votes to seven, with nine abstentions.'

# Cheryl Baker
Singer and Television Presenter

I was on tour with Bucks Fizz in its heyday. The tour was completely sold out and was going down a storm. Our stage show was always very colourful and involved lots of costume changes. Sometimes we only had thirty or forty seconds to change for the next song, as was the case on this particular occasion. I had to introduce 'The Rock Medley' and then had approximately forty seconds to completely change my clothes, shoes and jewellery, and put my hair up.

I ran offstage, put down my microphone, changed my clothes, took off my earrings and replaced them with a pair of diamantés. I slipped into my new shoes, put my hair up into a topknot and ran back on stage, with seconds to spare before my contribution to 'The Rock Medley'.

The spotlight focused on me and the audience started laughing. I was singing into my hairbrush!!

# Richard Baker

O.B.E., R.D.

Broadcaster and Author

In the days when I read the BBC TV News most evenings, my face was known to most of the population. One night I came out of the studio to be greeted by a small boy who said: 'Can I have your autograph?'

'Certainly,' I replied. 'Do you know who I am?'

'No,' he said, 'who are you?'

'I'm a newsreader.'

'Never mind,' said the boy sympathetically, 'newsreaders is good swaps!'

\*     \*     \*

I gave up reading the news at the end of 1982, and since that time I have been recognised less and less frequently, especially by the young.

In the foyer of a hotel recently, there was a young boy and a rather older woman who evidently *did* know who I was. She whispered to the boy, who came over to me and asked: 'Is your name Richard Baker?'

'Yes,' I replied.

'Do you know, my gran remembers you reading the news,' he said – which put me neatly in my place as one of the Old Brigade!

16

# Ian Bannen
Actor

Two golfers were waiting to tee off at the tenth hole. Suddenly, along the lane which passed that tee appeared a funeral cortege.

One player insisted that they pause in their game. He removed his hat and stood with bowed head while the hearse and following cars went by.

His partner was particularly impressed, as he remained in this attitude of prayer for several minutes, so he exclaimed, 'I'm very impressed – funerals seem to move you greatly!'

His pal, replacing his hat, replied, 'Well, I reckoned it was the least I could do, as I've been married to her for forty years!'

# Peter Barkworth
Actor, Director, Author

Mr Wilfred Murgatroyd's wife died, and he was terribly upset. He wanted her funeral to be very special, and particularly wanted her gravestone to be dignified and have a lovely message. He asked around and decided that a simple inscription:

SHE WAS THINE

would be very appropriate.

After the funeral the undertaker rang and said that the stone was ready, and he'd be delighted to take Mr Murgatroyd to the cemetery to see it. They arrived, and together they read:

TO THE MEMORY OF
MABEL MURGATROYD
DEARLY BELOVED WIFE OF
WILFRED

and then, underneath:

SHE WAS THIN

'Oh, look at that!' exclaimed Mr Murgatroyd. 'She was thin! You've left off the "E". "She was thine", that's what we wanted. Please have it put right; it's terribly upsetting.'

'I'm so sorry, Mr Murgatroyd,' said the undertaker. 'Stupid boy! I'll get him to put the "E" on today. Come and see it tomorrow. It'll be done then.'

So the following day Mr Murgatroyd went to inspect it, and read:

TO THE MEMORY OF
MABEL MURGATROYD
DEARLY BELOVED WIFE OF
WILFRED

and then, underneath, he read:

EE, SHE WAS THIN

# Carol Barnes
Television Journalist and Newscaster

In the days when communications were more primitive than they are today, and we all used to telex back from abroad, a distinguished ITN journalist covering the Vietnam war had the following exchange of communication with ITN in London.

He telexed: 'Money all gone. Please send five thousand pounds.'

The reply he received was: 'Your mission: cover Vietnam – not buy it!'

# Michael Barrymore
Entertainer and Television Personality

*Making a Bad Impression*

This story takes place on the road. I always used to listen to the London Independent radio station, LBC. In fact, one of the best times for me was late at night, whilst travelling back from cabaret appearances and television recordings.

This night was no exception. I was travelling with a mate of mine and we were listening to Clive Bull, a DJ who presented a phone-in show in the early hours of the morning. On this particular occasion, the phone-in was a talent contest on the radio! Listeners were invited to call the station and show off their talent, which was to be judged by a panel of 'experts'.

Well, I decided that I would enter the competition, just to see how talented I really was! So we pulled off the M25 and onto a trading estate. It was now well past midnight. The switchboard operator at LBC told me that they would be delighted for me to appear – I kept my identity secret by using an assumed name – but that she thought there might be a problem because I was using a mobile phone.

I quickly got my mate to scribble down an act for me to do. I would do impressions, we decided. I had about ninety seconds in which to perform. So I braced myself. I was on. . .

I opened with an impression of Danny La Rue, and worked my way through Loyd Grossman, Tommy Cooper, David Frost, and then finished off with myself. You won't believe how difficult it is to do an impression of yourself!

So this make-believe contestant finished his performance, and I began the drive back home, listening intently to LBC to hear the comments on my performance. It was a long wait, as I had to wait for the other contestants to perform first – there were ten in all.

Eventually, the moment came. The first expert liked my Danny La Rue! The second expert got a bit mixed up between my Loyd Grossman and my David Frost. But the third expert was devastating. Basically I was confident, she said. But my impressions were rusty. The whole performance had not impressed her and, worst of all, she thought my impression of Michael Barrymore was dreadful – it sounded nothing like him!

And to top it all, I came seventh out of ten!

# Raymond Baxter
Broadcaster and Writer

As a Christmas present, a cheese grater was sent to the blind Chairman of St. Dunstan's. He said it was the most violent book he had ever read!

# David Bellamy

Ph.D., F.L.S., F.I.Biol.
Botanist, Writer and Broadcaster

Have you heard the story of the two caterpillars crawling along a twig?

A butterfly flew past them, overhead.

One caterpillar said to the other: 'You will never get *me* up in one of those things!'

# David Benedictus

Writer, Director for Stage, Screen and Radio

I published a novel called *The Guru and the Golf Club* and suggested to my publishers that we launch it at a golf club, with a guru as a guest speaker.

I advertised for a guru, and the publishers booked Moor Park for a lunch for about thirty journalists. The guru who answered my advertisement looked extremely worldly. He wore an open-necked shirt and appeared to work at the Post Office, claiming to be 'on strike'. I expressed my concern to the publisher, who reassured me that he had acquired 'the real thing', which indeed he had – a most holy man in long saffron robes.

The photographers wanted a photograph of him driving off from the first tee. He refused, feeling it undignified, but was content to be photographed striding with his clubs down the fairway.

At the lunch he spoke on right-mindedness and associated topics for a very long time, while 'my' guru complained that at this rate it would be too late for him to collect his cheque from the dole office!

As the afternoon wore on, the journalists drifted away – leaving only the publishers, the two gurus and me. The book launch was *not* a success!

# John Birt
Director-General, BBC

*Lese-Majesty*

During the dark days of the last war, King Olaf of
Norway arrived at Broadcasting House, from where he
was to make a broadcast to the people of Norway. He
courteously greeted the commissionaire on duty in the
reception room and announced: 'I am the King of
Norway, and I am here to send a message to my
countrymen.'

Unabashed, the commissionaire said: 'Right you
are, Sir, I'll just check on the studio for you.' He picked
up the phone. 'Is that Studio 3? Only I've got the . . .'
He paused and enquired: '*Where* did you say you were
King of?'

# Rabbi Lionel Blue
Lecturer, Broadcaster, Author

At a rabbinical meeting, one of the rabbis mentioned that during the entire discussion no one had mentioned God once.

The rabbi next to me whispered in my ear, 'Namedropper!'

# Chris Bonington

C.B.E.

Mountaineer, Writer and Photographer

The European Everest Expedition in 1970 was made up of a number of German climbers and three Britons – Don Whillans, Doug Scott and Hamish MacInnes. They were all sitting at base camp, listening to the BBC overseas service, when the announcement was made that Germany had just defeated England in the World Cup Football Match.

Dr Karl Herrligkoffer turned to Don Whillans and said, 'Aha, we have beaten you at your national game.' Don Whillans, famous for his pugnacity and sharp one-liners, replied, 'Yes, but we've beaten you at your national game twice, 'aven't we?'

# Simon Brett
Writer, Radio Producer

There are occasions in all of our lives when we say something which cannot be unsaid. An inadvertent insult has slipped out and there's simply nothing we can do about it.

I remember being at a Christmas drinks party many years ago. I'd arrived early; the only other people present were my host and a girl I knew vaguely called Felicity. It being Christmas, the room was decorated with cards pinned to hanging ribbons. At the bottom of one strip was a card which I can remember to this day – home-made, silver-foil-covered, with a yellow feather attached by a blue sticker. To make conversation, I took hold of the card and observed to my host, 'Goodness, you've got some pretentious friends.' I then turned it over to read the message: 'Happy Christmas, lots of love, Felicity'!!

# Peter Cadbury
Industrialist, Philanthropist

The Devil and God were disputing the boundary between Heaven and Hell. Eventually, they decided to go to court and instruct their respective lawyers. After a long delay, St. Peter rang the Devil to explain that they could not go to court as there was no lawyer in Heaven!

\*   \*   \*

Patrick and Mick were taking a load of manure across a road in Ireland. They drove the horse and cart out of the farmyard without looking. Just then, a Ferrari shot down the main road at a hundred miles an hour. The driver, to avoid the horse and cart, swerved into the farmyard, turned over and burst into flames.

'Begorrah! It was lucky we got out in time!' exclaimed Patrick.

\*   \*   \*

The vicar saw a young girl struggling up the road with a cow. 'I'm taking her to the bull,' she told him.

'Can't your father do it?' the vicar asked.

'Oh no, dad says it has to be a bull.'

COTTAGE
DAIG
ERLOCH

30

# Dame Barbara Cartland

D.B.E., D.St.J.
Authoress, Playwright

*The Social Code*

Society through the centuries
Has evolved a social code,
Not written down but handed down
From the time we all wore wode.

For those who think they have blue blood,
There are rules of what to do.
The penalty of ignoring them
Is to be told, 'You're just non-U'.

So don't say 'cheers' when you have a drink,
Or hold your knife like a pen.
'Pardon' is a word which should never be heard,
And 'perfume' does not entice men.

So never 'phone' for a taxi
To take you 'up to town'.
And don't put clean wine glasses
On a cocktail tray – upside down.

Don't eat asparagus with a fork
Or put the milk in first.
Don't ask your guest 'to have a gin'
When he has a thirst.

Don't write to me on 'notepaper'
Or send me a 'photo', please.
Don't put 'née' in the births and deaths,
Or use pretty lace doilies.

Don't ask the way to 'the toilet', dear,
Or use a 'serviette'.

Men don't enter a restaurant first,
Or 'perspire' at the bill they get.

Don't have 'a lounge' in your lovely 'home',
Or open the 'bubbly' with glee.
Don't have gold-tipped party cards,
Or use little forks at tea.

You can do all these things if you wish,
And it doesn't matter a damn.
But they label you neatly as what you are,
Like a pickled herring can.

This poem is just asking for controversy! Having written a book on etiquette, I was on a David Frost Show with Professor Ross (who invented the expression 'U and non-U') and Mrs Betty Kenward, the social arbitress of good taste. We agreed on most things, except that the Professor said it was 'non-U' to say 'handbag'!

\*       \*       \*

*The Melon Story*

One of the first big dinner parties I went to when I left school was given at Arlington House by the fabulously rich Lady Michelham.

About thirty people sat down at a huge table which was covered in orchids and set with gold plates. I had never even seen gold plates before, let alone eaten off them!

The first course was a slice of Canteloupe melon. I picked up a gold spoon, but at the first touch the melon leapt off the plate and disappeared under the table.

I sat crimson with embarrassment while it was retrieved by a disdainful footman with powdered hair, and another piece placed in front of me!

# The Hon. Mr Justice Cazalet

A barrister-at-law, one of the greatest of his day, dies and goes to Heaven. When he arrives there, he asks, 'What is there to do in this place?'

St. Peter says, 'Well, you can handle some big court litigation cases. We've got six for you to take on.'

So the barrister says, 'What, six cases! Ready for trial?'

'Yes,' says St. Peter.

The barrister exclaims, 'That's wonderful! I'm really going to enjoy this! Tell me, how soon can I start?'

'In six months' time,' replies St. Peter.

The barrister groans, 'Six months! Why so long?'

St. Peter explains, 'Well, I'm afraid that's just the way it is. We have quite a backlog at the moment.'

So the Barrister decides, 'I can't wait that long. I'm going down to try at the other place.'

He goes down to Hell, sees the Devil there and announces himself. The Devil says, 'Well, I've got six cases for you to try.'

The barrister says, 'Six cases here for me to try?'

'Yes,' confirms the Devil.

Then the barrister says, 'Oh, this is great! When can I start the first trial?'

'Well,' says the Devil, 'you can start the first one tomorrow.'

'Oh!' exclaims the barrister, 'tomorrow! That's amazing! People can *really* go on trial here as soon as tomorrow? I was just up in Heaven and they said that I had to wait six months for the first trial! How come I can start so quickly here?'

'Oh,' laughs the Devil, 'that's easy! We've got a lot more judges down here!'

# Sebastian Coe

O.B.E., M.P.

Politician, Runner and Author

My first days in Parliament were an interesting introduction to traditional protocol. The new intake are thrown in at the deep end with little guidance or help.

On the very first day of Parliament I joined Gyles Brandreth for supper in the Members' Dining Room. As we entered, I spotted a small, empty table tucked away in the corner of the dining room, and we sat down. Moments later the Head Waiter came up to us and said: 'You are dining with the Chief Whip tonight?'

We made a rather swift exit!

# Paul Coia
Broadcaster, Television Personality and Presenter

Being a native of Glasgow, I was delighted to be invited back to the fair city to host the opening ceremony of the Special Olympics. This spectacular curtain-raiser for the 'Disabled Games', as they used to be known, was held at Celtic Park. The guests included Don Johnson and Melanie Griffith, Wet Wet Wet, Roxette, Frank Bruno, and many more.

Security was tight, since the crowned heads of Europe were present, and after the show we all mingled in the Jock Stein lounge. Prince Albert of Monaco chatted to sports stars; Queen Noor of Jordan spoke to Lisa Stansfield and others, and all the while the armed security men stayed resolutely in the background.

As you can tell, it was not conducive to feeling relaxed, having such well protected Royals there. However, one Glaswegian saw through the whole thing. He had been asked to look after travel arrangements for the day and arrived at the reception with one too many celebratory wines inside him.

He asked me which one of the guests was Queen Noor of Jordan. Apparently, her chauffeur-driven limousine had just arrived. So I pointed out the immaculately-coiffured head, and he staggered over. Not being able to get quite near enough because of security, our man was not for standing on protocol.

He shouted loudly, 'Hey! Queen Noor! Queen Noor!' until she turned around and then followed this up with, 'Hey Queenie! Yer taxi's here! Hurry up and don't keep him waiting!'

Her look of astonishment, as the transport manager staggered back to the bar, was priceless!

35

# Wendy Craig
Actress


The scene is a supermarket. A young mother is pushing her trolley down the aisle, and her five-year-old child is scouring the shelves for his favourites.

Suddenly he runs to a display, pulls out a package and runs back to her with it. She smiles tolerantly and says, 'No, Tommy, put it back; you have to *cook* that!'

# Barry Cryer
Writer, Broadcaster, Television Personality

My favourite story concerning an after-dinner speaker is the one about the speaker who declined expenses – the organiser said, 'Thank you. We'll put the money into our fund for better speakers.'

# Paul Daniels
Magician, TV Presenter & Personality

Did you know that fishing is the number one participation sport in the UK? Well, it is and that surprises most people. What most people do know, however, is that fishermen are prone to exaggerate the size of their catches.

Two such fishermen were doing what fishermen do best – propping up the bar and telling tales.

'I had a magnificent catch last week,' said one.

'I'll bet mine was better,' said the other.

'I caught a pike,' said the first, 'and it was so large that I needed a low-loader to take it home. It was nine-and-a-half feet long and weighed two-and-a-half tons. My line was only twenty-five pounds breaking strain, so I had to play the pike for fifteen hours to tire it out.'

The other fisherman listened to all this without batting an eyelid. A slightly raised eyebrow was enough to express a modicum of disbelief.

At last he spoke. 'I told you that my catch was better,' he said. 'Last week I was fishing in the Solent and I got something on the line that was so heavy that I thought the rod would snap. I eased and cajoled the line and the reel to bring it up out of the water. There, caught on the hook was an old ship's lantern in perfect condition. This lantern was obviously from an old Spanish galleon and it was incredibly ornate. It was probably 400 years old – and the candle was still lit.'

'Do you think I'm stupid or what?' asked the first fellow.

'No, I don't think you're stupid, so I'll tell you what we'll do. You cut eight feet off your pike and I'll blow my candle out!'

# Nigel Davenport
Actor

A tortoise was assaulted and robbed by three snails. Very shocked, the tortoise reported the attack at the police station. The police, who were very sympathetic, asked if the tortoise could give details and perhaps describe the assailants.

The tortoise replied: 'No, I'm sorry I can't. It all happened so fast!'

# Michael Denison

C.B.E.

Actor and Author

Lord Birkett was trying a little man who was not represented by counsel.

B.     'Would you like the services of counsel?'
L.M.   'No thank you, my lord.'
B.     'If you are concerned about the cost, don't let that worry you. You may choose from the learned counsel present – what is called a dock brief – and it need not cost you anything.'
L.M.   'No thank you, my lord.'

Well, you cannot force an accused to be represented. So the trial got under way. The prosecuting counsel outlined the case for the Crown and examined his first witness. When he had finished, Birkett asked the accused if he had any questions to put to the witness. 'No, my lord.' Nor had he any questions for any of the other witnesses.

This greatly accelerated the legal process and in no time the prosecuting council had made his closing speech; Birkett had summed up; the jury had retired; the jury had returned with a verdict of 'Guilty', and the clerk of the court asked the prisoner whether he had anything to say before sentence was passed. 'Yes,' he said – which caused a slight sensation, as they were by now used to him saying 'no'.

B.     'Well, what have you to say?'
L.M.   'It couldn't have been me, my lord.'
B.     'What do you mean, it couldn't have been you?'
L.M.   'Well, it couldn't.'
B.     'Why not?'
L.M.   'Because I was in prison at the time.'
B.     'Well, why didn't you say so?'
L.M.   'I thought it would prejudice my case!'

# Rachael Heyhoe Flint

M.B.E.

Journalist, Broadcaster, Public Speaker, Sportswoman, Writer

A cricket match was taking place in deepest rural Devon.

A village yokel walked out to bat with only one pad on. As he took his guard from the umpire, the highly observant umpire remarked to the yokel, 'You've only got one pad on!'

'Yes,' replied the yokel, 'we ain't got enough equipment in the club to go round all the team.'

'But you've got the pad on the leg furthest away from the bowler!' exclaimed the umpire.

'Ah,' declared the yokel, 'but I thought I was batting at the other end!'

# His Excellency Royce Frith
Canadian High Commissioner

The other day I met a friend who was walking down the street with his dog. I asked him where he was going with the dog. He replied that he was taking him to a dog show.

'That mutt?' I exclaimed. 'He couldn't win anything!'

'I know,' he said, 'but it introduces him to a better class of dog!'

# Bill Giles

O.B.E

Senior Weather Presenter at the BBC

Before the arrival of electronic graphics, we used to show paper satellite pictures. These were placed on a music stand with a camera locked on it. At the appropriate time we'd say, 'So let's look at the satellite picture,' and then pick up a knitting needle off camera, to point to it.

You had to be very careful because, being a bit nervous, your hand shook a little and the end of the needle moved from Southern England to Northern Scotland. If, however, you put the needle on the paper, you stood a good chance of ripping it!

On one occasion, a member of my staff (who shall remain anonymous – but it wasn't me, Michael Fish or John Kettley) said, 'Let's move to the satellite picture.' At that instant the camera failed, so the satellite picture wasn't shown. On the next broadcast he said, 'I'm determined to show you a satellite picture this time,' and opened his jacket to show one pinned onto the lining!

# Michael Grade
Chief Executive, Channel Four Television

'Thank you, Toastmaster, for that splendid introduction –
so much more elegant than a previous toastmaster, who
introduced me with the words, "My Lords, Ladies and
Gentlemen, pray for the silence of Mr Michael Grade!"'

# Tom Graveney

O.B.E.

International Cricketer

I was playing at Arundel in a National Playing Fields
Association game for the Duke of Norfolk's XI against the
Duke of Edinburgh's XI.

I went out to bat and had scored about fifteen, when
the Duke of Edinburgh came on to bowl his off-spinners
– he was quite a useful performer. He bowled one down
the leg-side, which I swept at and mistimed. The ball
lobbed out to mid-wicket, where the fielder caught me –
Wing Commander Chinnery, bowled H.R.H. You can't
get better than that!

I don't know whether it had any influence on future
events, but I was awarded the O.B.E. in the next New
Year's Honours List!!

# Lucinda Green

M.B.E.

Three-Day Event Rider,
Television Commentator, Writer


A substantial display of invitations, displayed on the
mantelpiece, is a good status symbol. The ruse is to print
your own – so the display looks good, but you do not
have the bother of going to any of them!

# Judith Hann
Writer, Broadcaster and TV Presenter

Two boys, who had absolutely hated each other at school, met on a railway station. It was over thirty years since they had last seen each other. Both had been successful; the portly bishop, dressed in his purple cassock, bristled when he recognised the lean admiral in full regalia.

'Excuse me, stationmaster,' said the bishop, 'is the train on time?'

'Certainly, madam,' replied the admiral, 'but I think that you should consider whether it is wise to be travelling in your condition!'

BARAVULLIN COTTAGE
LEDAIG
Nr. BENDERLOCH

# The Earl of Harrowby
T.D.

*Memorable Quotes*

'In Economics, the questions are always the same; it's the answers that change.'

'Just remember, Hubert, that if a speech is to be immortal it doesn't have to be eternal!'
— Muriel Humphrey, wife of USA Vice-President.

'We can see the enemy – and he is us!'
— American Cartoon Character

'Money can't buy friends. But you get a better class of enemy.'
— Spike Milligan

'The situation is critical, but not all that serious.'
— Irish

(On being told of the death of the impassive President Harding.) 'How could they tell?'
— Dorothy Parker

\*     \*     \*

Vienna, as you know, was the centre of the musical world in the 19th Century. There was full employment for all musicians. At the Congress of Vienna in 1815 the people of Austria watched the comings and goings of the Heads of State with growing concern. The story went round the City that:

> The Emperor of Russia loved for everyone.
> The King of Prussia fought for everyone.
> The King of Denmark spoke for everyone.

The King of Bavaria drank for everyone.
The King of Wurtenburg ate for everyone
and
The Emperor of Austria paid for everyone!

The national debt grew astronomically and the musicians
wrote the 'Luxury Tax Polka'!

# Lord Healey

C.H., M.B.E., P.C.

(Denis Healey)
Politician and Writer

When people complain about me wearing trainers, I always tell the story about the Frenchman and the Englishman who were on safari in the jungle. Suddenly, they were confronted by an angry lion. The Frenchman immediately put on his trainers, but the Englishman sneered, 'Don't be silly, you can't run faster than the lion!'

The Frenchman replied, 'I know, but that doesn't matter so long as I can run faster than you!'

# Jimmy Hill
BBC Television Personality and Sports Commentator


'. . . Julius Caesar is dead, Shakespeare's long gone, Einstein's left us relatively recently . . . and I'm not feeling too well myself!'

\*     \*     \*

'In the world of football you must have noticed how all the truly greats have been remembered by just one name: Cruyff, Best, Pele, Maradonna, etc. Let me introduce myself: I'm James William Thomas Hill and I used to play for Fulham!'

# David Jacobs

D.L.

Radio and Television Presenter, Author

*My Most Embarrassing Moment*

On a cold December night in the mid-70s I was asked to host a beauty competition in a South London cinema. When I arrived, I was rather saddened by the lack of beauty and also by the fact that the cinema was without central heating. However, I thought that by the time the show started a full house of enthusiastic spectators would warm the place up. Sadly, the event inspired only fifty people to attend – and they were mostly relatives of the contestants.

It was one of the dreariest pageants I have ever compered but, as a true professional, I tried to whip up as much enthusiasm as possible. The twelve contestants paraded in bikinis, their goose-pimples caused by the cold cinema doing nothing to enhance their beauty! When the time came and the judges had made their decision, I had the unenviable task of calling on the winner and runners-up in the time-honoured fashion of reverse order. When I announced the third and second, there was a mixture of whistles and cheers from the sparse audience.

And then came the moment everyone had been waiting for – the winner was to be announced. When I called out her number there were shrieks of derision from the assembled company, as on came quite the plainest girl of all. I looked at her in stunned shock, for I had called out No. 6 instead of No. 9 – my card was upside-down!

There was nothing for it but to reveal my mistake, whereupon No. 6 howled like a dying cat and No. 9 ran on – looking, I hasten to add, not all that much prettier but with a look of victory on her face and the requisite tears of joy.

Poor Miss No. 6! Poor me! I had to face the wrath of her family and fiancé – but that, as they say, is show business.

# Lionel Jeffries
Actor and Screen Writer

I must admit, I'm not sure what constitutes an after-dinner story. Any story, I suppose, told after dinner in order to raise an alcoholic laugh during a boring soliloquy from a bloated, self-satisfied guest of honour!

No – I don't enjoy after-dinner speakers, or formal dinners. In fact, I no longer attend them. My wife is the best cook ever, and home is where the laughs are.

However, here is an original limerick of mine:

> There once was a bishop of Crewe,
> Whose vestments were frilly and blue.
> As he walked through the doors
> There was a roar of applause –
> They thought it was Danny La Rue!

And a true incident:

I had appeared on a TV film and received a batch of excellent press reviews. As a consequence, I was really rather cocky. A few days later, whilst out shopping, I graciously accepted the occasional smile of recognition from the odd fan, and a few gushingly expressed: 'Loved the show, Lionel!'

(I must say, here and now, that I should have twigged right then – I never learn. The monster pride was taking over and I was due for the inevitable fall.)

Coming down the high street hill, a 'Hurrah Henry, *Country Life*' mum and her angelic six-year-old son approached me. He was tugging at the sleeve of her green, well-worn, waxed jacket.

'It's him, mummy! It is, it's him!'

'I don't think so, Christopher. He wouldn't be here in Saffron Walden. Actors don't do their own shopping.'

'It is him! Go on, ask for his autograph!'

At this, I reached for my Biro (an instant reaction to the very sound of 'autograph'). Children, bless them, are so discerning of talent and deserve due courtesy. They are, after all, your audience of the future. 'Grapple them to thy soul with hoops of steel' – when you're at the top of the ladder you may need them at the bottom! (Oh yes, pomposity and old man pride and me well and truly by the shorts.)

So I signed mum's shopping list:

'To Christopher, with love,
Lionel Jeffries'

and handed it to her.

She smiled, read, and frowned – yes she frowned! 'Oh dear – yes – well!'

'Wot? Something wrong? It is Christopher isn't it? You're Chris aren't you?'

'Christopher, yeth, not Chris.'

'No, it's not that! Oh, he's going to be frightfully disappointed!'

'Disappointed? Disappointed? Why disappointed?' I was slowly growing cold, like first-night nerves. Actors are incapable of handling life's realities. On stage, or in the studio, there is total control, but on LIFE's stage – disaster! The slightest hiccup in the unrehearsed events of everyday existence throws them into a state of high anxiety. The general public take it as being grand. It's not – it's panic!!

'Well – Leslie Jeffries – I mean, I don't want to be rude, but I've never heard of Leslie Jeffries.'

She *was* being rude.

'Lionel, madam, it's Lionel! Who the hell does he think I am?'

'There's no need to be nasty! My darling thought you were Wurzel Gummidge.'

'Wurzel Gummidge!!!'

'Yes, Christopher thought that's who you were – are.'

'I neither were nor are, Madam!'

I replaced my Biro, shaking, literally shaking, and huffed past them. Mistaken for another actor (Olivier, Grant, or even Caine) is hurtful enough – but a scarecrow!! The little swine.

The whole sad incident was some years ago. I've got over it now, of course . . .

# Peter Jones
Writer and Broadcaster

There was this beautiful convent in the South of France.
It overlooked the Mediterranean. There were olive trees
and mimosa all around. It was like living in paradise.
There was only one problem: a nun from the North of
England who indulged in bad language. It upset the
others and they remonstrated and begged her to desist.
But it was of no use – she just kept on effing and
blinding.

When the other sisters could stand it no longer, they
unburdened themselves to the Mother Superior. She was
a sweet old lady, beautiful and serene. She advised them,
'Pay no attention to these offensive words, but when our
unfortunate sister uses them, just walk quietly out of the
room. She will get the message eventually and mend her
ways.'

A few days later, four nuns were relaxing in the ping
pong room. The nun from the North of England walked
in and looked out across the bay. She saw warships.

'Ah,' she said, 'The bloody fleet's in.'

The four table tennis players laid down their bats and
moved towards the door.

The nun from the North shouted after them, 'There's
no need to hurry, they'll be here for a bloody fortnight!'

# Matthew Kelly
Actor, Broadcaster and Television Personality

I'll certainly never forget my first T.V. stunt. It happened thirteen years ago, at the start of the very first series of *Game for a Laugh*.

Before I became the presenter of the show I had been an actor – doing sitcoms and appearing on *Punch Lines*. But I liked trying new things and, when the producer asked me if I'd be prepared to jump out of a plane, I said a loud 'Yes'. Although I'd never been particularly sporty, maybe there was a secret daredevil lurking somewhere. Anyway, I'd have said yes to anything to get the job! And I got it, so I had to jump at Aldershot with the Red Devils.

My first two jumps, filmed for the show, were fine. I was terrified beforehand, of course – I always am – but when you work with service people they are terrific because they acknowledge fear and talk you through every detail.

Unfortunately, my beginner's luck went to my head. I was hooked. I wanted to jump again and even learn how to free fall. However, as I'd done my bit for the show and wasn't insured for any further leaps, I was told very strictly not to go back to the airfield. I said, 'O.K. I won't.' But I did.

The first jump was a success, but I wanted one more go. I went up in the air again and chatted to one of the Red Devils about how scary it is when you're landing and see the ground rushing up towards you at breakneck speed.

'Don't worry,' he said, 'just close your eyes, Matthew.' And I did. I hadn't realised he'd been joking.

I broke my leg in fourteen places! You could hear the crack all over the field. But that wasn't all. The regimental sergeant major, Malcolm Simpson – a brilliant bloke – was coming down just behind me. When he saw

I was in trouble, he blew his own jump, broke his wrist and damaged his kidneys. We were taken in the same ambulance to the Military Hospital in Cambridge. There, we were put in adjacent beds.

I was in agony and feeling very sorry for myself – but how I admired the sergeant major. He looked so cheerful and cool as he puffed away on a cigarette.

That night, I felt like calling the nurse every five minutes. However, Malcolm so impressed me that I thought, 'O.K. I'm in *real* man's territory here – I mustn't be a wimp!' So I suffered in silence.

The next morning I said to him, 'You were so brave last night – I was desperate to ring for the nurse.'

'So was I,' he laughed, 'but I couldn't find the bell!'

# Angela Knight, M.P. for Erewash

This Grace usually goes down well. It is a humorous start to a dinner and puts the audience in a cheerful frame of mind for the speaker who comes afterwards:

'God give us the power to eat this lot in half an hour.'

# Sue Lawley
Broadcaster

I remember the fate of a good friend of mine who was happily married to a successful working woman. At the end of a long day at the office, he wasn't feeling too well and decided to go and visit his doctor. After a thorough examination, the doctor told him: 'Charlie, I'm sorry to tell you this – but you've only got twelve hours to live.'

Charlie was, of course, shaken. But, pulling himself together, he drove back through the winter rain to his house and his waiting wife. The traffic was terrible, and on the way he thought about his limited future. When he arrived home, his wife took one look at him and said, 'Charlie, you look ghastly! What's the matter?'

Charlie replied, 'Darling, something awful has happened. I wasn't feeling well, so I went to see the doctor on my way home. He told me that I'd only got twelve hours to live. Well, actually, I've had such a terrible journey home that now it's only ten.'

'Oh, Charlie, my sweetheart, that's terrible!'

'Don't worry, darling,' said Charlie, 'I've been thinking on the way home what we should do. Let's put a bottle of our best Bollinger in the freezer to chill quickly while we light a lovely log fire. Then, when it's ablaze, we'll sit down and sip champagne and talk about the life we've had together. After that, I'll have eight hours left – so what we can do is grill a couple of fillet steaks and I'll open that bottle of 1970 Chateau La Fite which I've been keeping in the cellar. We'll enjoy a ravishing meal together and then I'll have six hours left. Then, darling, we'll go upstairs and make passionate love until, finally, with only half an hour or so to go . . . I'll fall asleep and die in your arms, a fulfilled and happy man.

'Mmm . . . Mmm,' replied his wife. 'It's all very well for you darling, but I've got to get up in the morning.'

# The Rt. Revd. and Rt. Hon. Dr Graham Leonard

K.C.V.O., P.C.
Bishop of London, 1981–91
Author

After his appointment as Bishop of London, one of my predecessors was taking leave of the diocese where he was then serving. This required his presence at many occasions when he had to reply to those who drank to his health and wished him well.

He felt that his supply of material was beginning to run out, and at one dinner he hoped to use a particular story on a later occasion as well. So he turned to the journalists who were present and asked them if, when reporting the event, they would not include that story.

Next day he read in the local paper: 'At this point in his speech the Bishop told a story which we are sorry we are unable to print.'

'Game set and match to the press' was his reaction.

# The Rt. Hon. Peter Lilley
M.P., P.C.

Secretary of State for Social Security, 1995–

A young Englishman was sitting in a Parisian restaurant and there was a pretty young girl at the table next to him. In an effort to initiate a conversation with her, he leaned over and said, *'Il y a une moustique dans votre salade!'*

She looked at him and replied in perfect English, 'I think you mean *"un" moustique.'*

Whereupon he exclaimed, 'My God, your eyesight must be good!'

# The Rt. Hon. Earl of Limerick

K.B.E., D.L., M.A.

Here are a couple of responses given by schoolboys to examination questions:

Challenged in a Religious Education paper to write down what he knew about Lot's wife, a schoolboy replied: 'Lot's wife was like unto other women until Lot turned and gazed upon her, whereupon she turned to a pillar of salt – by day, and a ball of fire by night.'

\*     \*     \*

An essay paper included the question, 'Which is worse – ignorance or indifference? Discuss.'

The response was relevant and concise, but nevertheless was marked down on the discussion element: 'I don't know, and I don't care!'

**ALBANY APARTMENTS
OBAN**

# Maureen Lipman
Actress, Broadcaster and Author

I've been doing a bit of speechmaking recently. Raising
the old profile for the odd buck for a good cause. It's an
effort, it's often time-consuming and nerve-jangling, but
it's never without interest. As Joyce Grenfell once said,
'You learn a lot – most of it good for the work, all of it
good for the soul.'

I often begin the speech by saying, 'Don't I look
thinner in real life?' It's *true*. I do. Much. It gets a hugely
affirmative response and pre-empts them whispering the
fact to each other! It also seems to break the ice quite
nicely too. (There is a story of the actress sister of Gladys
Cooper, who gave up show business because every time
she came on stage the audience seemed to be hissing at
her. In actual fact, what they were doing was whispering
to one another, 'She's Gladys Cooper's sister. She's
Gladys Cooper's sister . . .'!)

Basically, my job is: to know enough and care enough
about the designated charity; to effectively do a balancing
act between laughter and pain, and to use one to benefit
the other. In other words, I'm there to make the audience
laugh so much that their handbags fall open!

# Bryan Magee
Writer and Broadcaster

Two stories about political figures of different countries and centuries:

The Earl of Sandwich once said to the great 18th Century radical, John Wilkes, 'Sir, I don't know whether you'll die of the pox or on the gallows.'

To which, Wilkes replied, 'That depends on whether I embrace your principles or your mistress.'

\*　　\*　　\*

In America in the 1980s, a journalist once said to Nancy Reagan, 'Madam President, do you have anything to say to us on the subject of Red China?' To which she replied, 'Definitely – never, *never* with a yellow tablecloth!'

# Lady Olga Maitland

M.P.

Politician and Journalist

During the canvassing period leading up to the election in 1992, my husband, Robin, was out on the road with me, doing his bit. We were scattered about in different roads, and Robin and one of the constituency helpers called on one particular house. The lady there was not at all happy with the Conservative Party and proceeded to say why.

After some time, she said, 'Anyway, I don't like the look of this Lady Olga Maitland. Do you know her?'

Undaunted, Robin replied, 'As a matter of fact I have been married to her for over twenty years!'

'Well,' came the reply, 'more fool you!'

# Christopher Martin-Jenkins

Cricket Correspondent to The Daily Telegraph,
Author

This story concerns a sixteen-year-old girl being
questioned by her mother about what happened on her
first date.

'What did you do after the cinema?' asked the mother.
'We went out in his car,' said the daughter.
'What happened?' asked the mother.
'We stopped at that beauty spot at the top of the hill,'
replied the daughter.
'What happened then?' asked the mother.
'He put his hand on my knee,' said the daughter.
'What did you do?' asked the mother.
'I laughed,' said the daughter.
'What happened then?' asked the mother.
'He put his hand on my bosom,' said the daughter.
'What did you do?' asked the mother.
'I laughed,' said the daughter.
'What happened then?' asked the mother.
'He put his hand on my lap,' said the daughter.
'What did you do?' said the daughter.
'I laughed,' said the daughter.
'Why did you keep laughing?' asked the mother.
'Because the sweets were in my handbag!'

\*       \*       \*

A busy and ambitious young executive had been newly
appointed to a post in a large company. He arranged
meetings with all his staff on his first day in the office,
starting at 9 am sharp.

As the first man entered the anteroom of his office, he
picked up the phone and said in a loud voice, 'Make sure
I travel on Concorde next time – and make sure that the
champagne is cooler, is that understood? I don't want

warm champagne again. Oh, and another thing, I want those shares sold by lunchtime. If they're not sold at 225 by 2 pm this afternoon there will be trouble, got it?' And he put down the phone.

As he did so, he extended his arm to the first member of his staff and said, 'Good morning! I am John Smith, your new manager. How do you do?'

The other man said, 'Good morning! I'm Reg Perkins from British Telecom. I've come to connect your new phone.'

# Leo McKern

A.O.

Actor and Writer


Most of my best stories are, of course, hardly fit for your publication, but as this one is told in one of 'Inspector Forst's' books, perhaps it is innocent enough.

'Ah!' murmurs the vicar as the coffin containing the former mother of eighteen children is lowered, 'Together at last!'

The man beside him whispers indignantly, ''ere, wotcher mean, vicar? – I'm 'er 'usband and I'm still 'ere!'

'No, no,' replies the vicar, 'I was simply referring to your dear wife's legs!'

# Sir David McNee

K.St.J., Q.P.M.

Commissioner Metropolitan Police, 1979–82

The police, like all good, professional organisations, insist on a vigorous examination of a constable's professional competence before promotion. To test their knowledge of the law, administrative procedures, police regulations, judgement and leadership ability, each candidate for promotion is expected to answer a series of problems. These problems are designed to reflect the type of everyday practical incidents which confront police officers on the streets.

The complexity of some of these questions has become the butt of police humour, and one police joker composed a question which went as follows:

> You are on patrol when an explosion occurs in a gas main in a nearby street. On investigation, you find that a large hole has been blown in the footpath and there is an overturned van lying a few yards away. Inside the van are a man and a woman. Both are injured. You recognise the man as a disqualified driver and the woman as the wife of your inspector who is presently on a course at the police college. There is a strong smell of alcohol inside the van.
>
> A passing motorist stops to give you assistance and you recognise him as a man who is wanted for armed robbery.
>
> At that moment a man runs out of a house, shouting that his wife is expecting a baby and the shock of the explosion has started birth prematurely.
>
> You then notice that a man is crying for help, having been blown into an adjacent canal by the explosion. He cannot swim.

In addition, there are two dogs fighting in the street. Neither is wearing a collar.

A group of men standing in the doorway of a public house – drinking after hours and shouting drunken encouragements – are urging the dogs to fight.

Bearing in mind the provisions of the Mental Health Act and the fact that you are due to appear on a disciplinary charge initiated by your inspector, describe in a few words what action you would take.

It is alleged that a bright young officer scratched his head, thought for a moment, picked up his pen and wrote:

'Remove uniform and mingle with crowd.'

# The Rt. Hon. David Mellor
Q.C., P.C., M.P.

I am often asked to speak at events where there are, in my audience, people who are almost certainly better qualified to speak than I am. On these occasions, I tell them I feel a little like the minor Italian composer who was much moved by the death of Rossini.

So moved was he that he composed a funeral anthem to be performed at a memorial service to the great man. Afterwards, like all creative artists, he was keen to know how it had gone. So he approached a fellow composer and asked, 'What did you think of my anthem?'

The other composer looked embarrassed, shuffled his feet, stared at the ground and, after a long pause, finally replied, 'Well, perhaps it might have been better if *you* had died and *he* had written the music!'

# Dr. Patrick Moore

C.B.E., F.R.A.S.

Astronomer, Broadcaster and Freelance Author

The vote-catching politician was on a tour of Africa. He went to the first village and made an impassioned speech: 'We will give you houses! We will give you pensions! Vote for me!'

The whole audience was wildly enthusiastic, and shouted: '*Kabala! Kabala!*'

On he went to the next village and made the same speech, with the same reception: '*Kabala! Kabala!*'

It was the same everywhere, and he was greatly encouraged.

Finally, he arrived at a village where the head man had actually been to Oxford. Same speech; enthusiastic audience shouting '*Kabala! Kabala!*' and it seemed that all was well.

This was the end of the tour, and he had dinner with the head man in his mud hut. 'Jolly good show, old boy,' remarked the head man. 'Sorry you have to go. Anything you want to do while you're here?'

The politician nodded. 'Yes, indeed. As you know, I'm very keen on culture and I know there's a fascinating old temple near here. Do you think I could go and see it?'

The head man nodded. 'Certainly, old boy. Nothing is easier. I'll take you there tomorrow. One thing, though. You must put on your gum-boots because this is the temple of our sacred bull – and it's knee-deep in *kabala!*'

# Michael Noakes
P.P.R.O.I., R.P.

Landscape and Portrait Painter

The scene is the main staircase of the Royal Academy. I was a very young painter, with a modest picture hanging in an obscure corner of the annual Summer Exhibition.

As I mounted the steps on Varnishing Day, I met a senior member of the R.A., whom I knew slightly. 'Nice Exhibition!' said he.

'Thank you . . .' I replied!

\*　　\*　　\*

It was the mid-Seventies, and I was painting the Queen in the Yellow Drawing Room at Buckingham Palace. I had noticed that the usual small silver tray with a bottle of Malvern Still Mineral Water and a couple of glasses had not been put there ready for possible use, and I was disappointed because I always felt ready to engulf a glass or two after a sitting was over.

I gave it no more thought though, and the session was well underway when there was a tap at the door. One is normally never interrupted, so it was with irritation in my voice that – forgetting it was not my palace – I found myself calling out, 'Come in!'

A servant entered with the tray, and I rather curtly indicated that he should put it on the side. He did, and went away again. The Queen very kindly gave no hint that she had noticed I had forgotten that I was not in my own studio, and we continued with the sitting.

Two minutes later there was yet another tap at the door. This time I really made no attempt to contain my explosion of rage. 'Oh! Good grief! Who is it *now*!' I demanded. A young man put his head round the door and asked, very apologetically, if he could please just have a word with the Queen . . .

It was the Prince of Wales!

# Denis Norden

C.B.E.

Scriptwriter and Broadcaster

In an essay answer, an American naval cadet wrote:
'Sancho Panza always rode by the side of Don Quixote
on a burrow.' (Spelling it B.U.R.R.O.W.)

The instructor deducted marks for this and wrote in
the margin: 'A B.U.R.R.O. is an ass. A B.U.R.R.O.W. is
a hole in the ground. As a future naval officer, you are
expected to know the difference.'

# John Julius Norwich
C.V.O.
Writer and Broadcaster


The story that has given me the most pleasure is one that I read of a year or two ago in the *Daily Mail*. It concerned a family who tried to sue the Kensal Green Crematorium.

Apparently, the grandfather, who had recently died, had requested in his will that at the cremation service they should play a recording of 'Every Time You Say Goodbye'. Unfortunately the Crematorium put on the wrong side of the record and played 'Smoke Gets in Your Eyes'!

# The Rt. Hon. Lord Parkinson
P.C.
Politician and Writer

One of my favourite after-dinner stories is the one about the two old ladies who went shopping at Harrods on the first cold day of the year. Each of them was wearing a fur coat.

As they came out of Harrods, they were approached by an animal rights protestor, who said to one of the ladies, 'Madam, have you ever considered what poor little creature had to die so that you could be warm in that fur coat?'

The lady thought for a moment and replied, 'Yes, it was my mother-in-law.'

# Richard Pasco

C.B.E.

Actor of Stage, Screen and Television

Anecdote on the birth of his son by a Chinese poet who lived in the 8th Century:

> Families, when a child is born,
> Want it to be intelligent.
> I, through intelligence
> Having wrecked my whole life,
> Only hope the baby will prove
> Ignorant and stupid.
>
> Then he will crown a tranquil life
> By becoming a cabinet minister

# Bill Pertwee
Actor and Writer

A cricketer's wife was bringing a charge of adultery against her husband. Her solicitor fixed a date at the magistrates' court for the first hearing.

In court the magistrate asked the wife, 'On what *grounds* are you bringing this charge against your husband?'

The lady replied, 'Lords, Trent Bridge and The Oval.'

# Frederic Raphael
Author

Randolph Churchill was a man who did not hesitate to say boo to geese. He was capable of bullying the great, which is admirable, and also of bullying those whom he considered underlings, which is less so.

At one time he contributed regularly to the *Daily Express*, at a period when it was the most successful newspaper in Fleet Street. The sub editors were, perhaps, the most important people in the newsroom, since they shaped and formed the style of the paper. They were like the sergeant majors in a Guards regiment, and not easily intimidated.

One day, Randolph came swaggering in and began to bully one of the female secretaries who had, he alleged, mistyped his work. He ranted and roared and dared anyone to challenge his stridency.

When he had more or less reduced the girl to tears, one of the 'subs' turned round and said, 'You know your trouble, Churchill? Your name begins with C.H. in *Who's Who* and S.H. in What's What.'

*  *  *

There is no record of the sub's name, but it is one of the great anonymous remarks of all time – equalling, perhaps, that of Diogenes, the Cynic philosopher (who, so it is said, lived in a barrel).

Diogenes was famous enough to be visited by Alexander the Great, at the height of his renown. Alexander came to the 'door' of his barrel and asked Diogenes whether there was anything in the world he could do for him.

Diogenes did not look up. He simply said, 'You could always move out of the way; you're blocking the light.'

# His Excellency Moshe Raviv
Ambassador of Israel

A man fell in love with a lady and was so enamoured with her that he wrote her a love letter every day.

After a year, the lady could not resist marrying the postman!

# Lord Renton

P.C., K.B.E., Q.C.
Politician and Philanthropist

When a Conservative government was elected in 1951, the Leader of the House of Commons, Mr Harry Cruickshank, was asked at question time whether, after six years of socialist government, the new government had found any skeletons in the cupboards of Whitehall.

'Oh, no,' he replied, 'They were hanging from the chandeliers!'

\*       \*       \*

The Secretary of State for Scotland in that government, James Stuart, was opening a debate on Scottish affairs and was asked to speak up. He replied, 'I am most awfully sorry but I did not know anyone was listening!'

# Sir Julian Ridsdale

C.B.E.

Politician and Specialist on Japanese,
European and American Affairs


When my eldest grandson was five years old we invited
round for Christmas a Japanese couple who had close
connections with the Imperial Family. They brought with
them their son, who was about the same age as my
grandson.

To welcome them, my grandson held out his hand to
the friends' son. But instead of shaking his hand, the boy
bowed to my grandson who, without hesitation, kissed
him on the top of his head.

Leave it to the children to show the real way to make
friends!

# Lord Rix

C.B.E., D.L.

Reprinted from *Tour de Farce* (published by Hodder Headline)
Written with Elspeth, Lady Rix

Early in his career, Leslie Crowther was appearing at the Fol-de-Rols in Scarborough, staying in digs with an outside privy. Just after midnight he was caught short. He was making his uncertain way to one of two outside loos when suddenly a window was flung open and there, silhouetted in the pitiless glare of a 100 watt bulb, was his landlady.

'Mr Crowther, are you going to the lavatory?'

Mr Crowther assured her that he was.

'Well, don't go in that one, luv; it's next door's and we're not speaking.'

\*　　\*　　\*

Was it not the French statesman, de Richelieu, who discovered his wife in bed with her lover and remarked: 'Madam, you really must be more careful. Suppose it had been someone else who found you like this!'

\*　　\*　　\*

When one old actor was asked if he thought that Hamlet had ever slept with Ophelia, he considered for a moment and then said, with a certain degree of nostalgia:

'On tour, yes. In the West End, never!'

# Willy Russell
Author and Dramatist

After-dinner speaking is something I normally avoid at all costs. However, a couple of months ago I was telephoned by my friend and colleague Alan Bleasedale, who was booked to speak at a dinner for 200 head teachers. Unfortunately, Alan's filming commitments in Ireland were such that he could not honour the engagement. So he telephoned to ask if I would stand in for him. Knowing that in similar circumstances Alan would do the same for me, I agreed.

In a discussion with the host for the evening, it was agreed that rather than present an after-dinner speech, I would instead read from a novel I am currently writing. The novel in question is written in the form of letters – that is, it is an epistolary novel.

As I rose from my chair to address the assembled head teachers, it suddenly occurred to me that during my preamble I could affect the style and tone of a headmaster myself. When, in the introduction, I used the word epistolary, I suddenly pointed to one of the head teachers sitting towards the back of the room and (as if he were a kid in a classroom), I exclaimed, 'Epistolary! You lad! Epistolary, what does it mean?'

To my absolute horror (and no doubt to his) the head teacher concerned looked totally blank. Not having intended to embarrass anyone, and quickly seeking to shift the attention away from my intended victim, I scanned the entire room and demanded, 'Epistolary! Come on, can any of you tell me what it means?' Two hundred nervous and sheepish faces looked blankly back at me!

Perhaps it's just as well that I don't normally give after-dinner speeches!

# Sir Peter Saunders

Producer of the world's longest running play *The Mousetrap* and over 100 others. Former Film Director, Journalist and Author

I had a theatre manager who was very efficient – but I was certain he was up to no good. Yet I couldn't catch him out.

One day I sent for him and said, 'Mr D. Here is a letter for you to sign, resigning from your job and accepting £1,000 in full compensation.'

Looking at him very meaningfully, I said, 'We both know *why*, don't we Mr D.?'

The manager went ashen white and signed. And to this day I don't know what he had been doing!

# David Shepherd
O.B.E., F.R.C.D., F.R.G.S.
Wildlife Artist and Conservationist

When you come to think about it, it doesn't make much sense to walk up to two wild elephants in Africa with a full-scale studio easel, tubes of oil paint, brushes, and an enormous gleaming white canvas, expecting them to stand still for five days while you paint their portraits!

However, this is almost exactly what we did a few years ago when the BBC decided to make a fifty-minute documentary featuring my life as a wildlife artist, specialising, as I do, in elephants.

We were quite a party as we went into Zambia's Luanga Valley National Park. We needed two landrovers to carry us all: we had two game wardens to look after us in case of problems; I had all my painting equipment; my wife was with me, and we had the whole television team – the producer with his notes, the programme secretary, the cameraman, the assistant cameraman, the sound recordist with his microphone, and also a couple of Africans to look after us. If tourists in another landrover had come round the corner to see all those people walking up in a long line to two unsuspecting elephants under a tree, they would have no doubt thought that everybody in Zambia was completely mad!

By walking up very, very quietly, we got to within a few paces of the two elephants, who had no idea we were there. Giggling very quietly to myself with excitement, all I could hear was the whirring of the movie camera behind me. We got some amazing footage.

The next day we tried again. However, this time we were charged at by a very angry cow elephant! My wife and I had to run like the clappers back to the landrover. When I looked over my shoulder, I saw the game warden standing his ground. I am sure that cow elephant spoke perfect English. She stopped dead in her tracks, shocked at the outpouring of obscene four-letter words directed at her! Sketching elephants in the wild is not something I would recommend!

# Lord Stafford

D.L.

The following story happened to me not long after my father died and I inherited the title.

I went to a garage to buy some spare parts for the car. The young boy behind the counter asked me what my name was, so I replied, 'Mr Lord Stafford.' A moment later I corrected myself, 'No, it is Lord Stafford.'

He then wrote down 'Lloyd Stafford'.

I said, 'No, I'll write it,' and I wrote down 'Lord Stafford'.

He then turned round and asked 'What's that – isn't it a pub?'

# Lord Stevens of Ludgate
Chairman of United Newspapers PLC

A man goes into a shop and says, 'I'd like to buy a parrot.'

The shopkeeper says, 'Well, we've got three parrots; which one would you like?'

The customer points to one and asks, 'How much is that one?'

'One thousand pounds,' replies the shopkeeper.

'My goodness!' says the customer, 'That's a lot of money!'

'Well,' says the shopkeeper, 'that parrot speaks fluent French and Italian.'

'Nevertheless,' says the man, 'it costs too much for me. How much is that one?'

'That one is two thousand pounds,' says the shopkeeper.

'My goodness!' exclaims the customer, 'What on earth does that one do?'

The shopkeeper answers, 'That one speaks fluent Korean, Malay, Japanese and Chinese. And,' he says, 'before you ask, the third one is three thousand pounds.'

'My God!' exclaims the customer, 'What in heaven's name does he do?'

'I don't know,' replies the shopkeeper, 'but the other two call him "Chairman"!'

# Alastair Stewart

Television Journalist, Newscaster and Correspondent

In 1982 I was filming for ITN in St. Peter's Square, Rome, hoping to catch a word with His Holiness the Pope about his proposed visit to Great Britain. The problem was that Britain, a Protestant country, was at war (over the Falklands) with Argentina – a Roman Catholic country. These were trying times.

We hired a local cameraman in Rome, because that was cheaper. As His Holiness approached, I prepared myself for my big moment: would I get the question out, loud and clear? Would the Pope see and hear me? Would he give me an answer? These were tense moments.

Slowly, he approached, getting nearer and nearer. I drew in my breath and drew myself up to my full height.

'Your Holiness,' I began. And just at that moment the Roman cameraman, a good Catholic lad, saw the Pope in his viewfinder. He immediately went down on one knee before his spiritual leader on earth.

I had hoped for a perfectly framed picture of the Pope, telling me he WOULD come to Britain. Instead, I got the words – but they will forever be accompanied by a perfectly focused picture of the papal slippers!

# Chris Tarrant
Broadcaster and Television Personality

I was filming one week down in Herefordshire. It was a diabolical week, bitterly cold and pouring with rain most of the day, which made life pretty miserable and filming downright impossible. After about four days of hanging about our hotel, getting smashed out of our brains every night and soldiering through the very same menu every lunch and dinner time, I was invited by the very nice lady whom I was eventually supposed to interview – a retired schoolmistress – to have dinner with her and her husband, just to break the monotony.

I got myself spruced up and knocked on their very large front door at seven-thirty on the dot. Patricia came out smiling to me. She produced a large Scotch from a beautiful antique drinks cabinet and motioned me into the lounge.

'Charles is in by the fire,' she said. 'Go and say hello while I serve up. But whatever you do, don't touch his nose.'

I stared at her departing back with my mouth opening and closing. What? Don't touch his nose? I mean, it had never crossed my mind! Why on earth would I go up to some complete stranger and touch his nose, anyway?

I walked into the lounge and there, beaming amiably in front of the fire, was Charles. He is a great big bear of a man, about 6ft 5in, and used to play rugby for London Welsh. Charles is terribly well spoken and kindness itself.

'Nice to meet you, Chris,' he said. 'Got a drink have you? Good. Come on and sit down.'

Now all this polite chatting and handshaking was all very well, and I made suitably polite replies but, really and truly, all I wanted was to ask him about his nose. What was wrong with it? Why couldn't I touch it? I kept staring at it. It looked all right – a little large perhaps, but not broken or anything, no bandage.

Then the food arrived, which was really excellent after the meagre fare I'd been getting. The wine flowed freely and we all three got on like rabbits in a field of wet turnips. Charles has a really silly sense of humour, and his wife is lovely. But all the time, in the back of my mind, I kept hearing this one warning voice, ringing in my brain again and again: 'Whatever you do, don't touch his nose.'

The whole thing was absurd. Perhaps I'd misheard her; perhaps she'd said 'rose' or 'hose'. but that was even sillier. No, I hadn't misheard and, although nothing had been further from my mind when I had walked into their house that evening, by the end of dinner I wanted to touch his nose more than anything else in the world.

The brandy was passed round, the cigars came out. Charles and I sat next to each other, roaring with laughter and slapping each other on the back – until eventually, at about two o'clock in the morning, I could restrain myself no longer. As Charles sat rocking with laughter, I reached across the table, gently grabbed both nostrils between thumb and forefinger, and gave his nose a damn good tweaking.

There was a scream from Patricia and a crash of broken glass. Charles let out the roar of a wounded bull elephant. There was a great flash in front of my face and I vaguely made out the shape of a huge, hairy fist.

The next thing I remember is lying on the floor under the dinner table, tasting blood in my mouth, and a terribly apologetic Charles looming down over me, saying: 'I'm terribly sorry, old boy, but surely Patricia warned you. . .!!'

# Leslie Thomas
Author and Dramatist

A small boy was being taken around an art gallery by his mother. They passed before Canaletto's painting *The Adoration of the Magi,* and the mother explained the scene – the child Jesus in the manger, Mary and Joseph, the various farm animals and the Three Wise Men.

The boy was very puzzled as to why the Son of God should be born in such poor conditions.

'It is because his earthly parents had no money,' explained his mother.

The boy replied: 'They must have had some money to have their picture painted by Canaletto!'

# Bill Tidy
Cartoonist, Writer, Playwright,
Television and Radio Presenter


I was the after-dinner speaker at the gathering of the
Association of Clinical Biochemists in the Birmingham
Metropole Hotel. The event was organised by a young
lady and, when I arrived in the afternoon to look at the
room, I could see that she was extremely nervous.

I took her on one side and said paternally, 'Don't
worry, the room will be ready in time. The diners are all
upstairs showering after a good day's golf in the
sunshine and your after-dinner speaker is here on time.
There is no more cause for anxiety. Go upstairs and put
your party frock on.'

She looked at me bleakly and said, 'This *is* my party
frock!'

# Alan Titchmarsh
Television Personality, Broadcaster and Gardener

In the days of *Breakfast Time*, when the red sofa ruled supreme, I'd just finished a live gardening item, during which I was extolling the virtues of manure – having taken along a bucket of the sfuff and pushed my hands into it, to show how crumbly and delectable it was.

As the programme credits rolled, I started to scrape this wonderful brown soil enrichment from my hands, only to hear the programme producer saying to some unseen person: 'Don't shake hands with him – you've seen where they've been.'

I looked up in time to see The Princess of Wales walking towards me with hands outstretched. We met with a gentle squidge and, as our hands parted, the only thing I could think of to say was, 'I'll never wash again.'

# Lord Vestey

One of my favourite stories is about the time when famous racehorse trainer Jeremy Tree was asked to address the Eton College Racing Society (his old school). He was extremely excited and could not wait to tell someone about it.

The next day he met Lester Piggott on the racecourse and asked him what he thought he should tell the Society.

Lester Piggott replied: 'Tell them you've got flu.'

# Terry Waite
C.B.E.
Writer

The Pope decided to take a weekend away from the responsibilities of office. He boarded a plane, and several hours later stepped off at Kennedy Airport, New York. As he had only hand baggage, he walked through customs and went directly to dial a limo. The limo duly arrived.

The Holy Father looked at his watch. 'I need to be at St. Patrick's in three quarters of an hour,' he said to the driver.

'Are you crazy, bud?' responded the New Yorker. 'It's Friday night; it's raining; it's rush hour. It's impossible!'

'Nothing is impossible,' said the Pope. 'You get in the back and I shall drive.'

'OK by me,' said the driver, and he promptly disappeared behind the rear darkened windows.

The Pope got behind the wheel and set off at seventy-five miles per hour. He had only been travelling for about three minutes when a traffic cop pulled him over. He took one look at the driver and got on his radio.

'Hey Lieutenant,' he said, 'I've just pulled a guy for speedin'.'

'What's new?' came the reply.

'This guy is a very important guy,' responded the cop.

'How important? More important than the President?'

'Sure', said the cop, 'he's more important than the President.'

'How do you know he's more important than the President?'

'Well,' said the cop, 'he must be. The Pope's driving him!'

# Ian Wallace

Singer, Actor and Broadcaster

Many years ago, an English opera singer was invited to sing the part of Mephistopheles in Gounod's opera *Faust* in a small theatre in Ireland.

He was, of course, a bass. Now one of the problems about being a bass singer in opera is that you never get the girl. You're either the villain, a monk or that fate worse than death, the hero's friend. The nearest you ever get to the soprano is to give her a chaste kiss on the brow in Act 3, to console her for something the tenor did to her in Act 2. Sometimes, of course, your part is funny, but not if you're singing Mephistopheles – until this singer made history.

When he arrived for rehearsals he noticed that there was an old-fashioned trap door at centre stage. You know, the sort of thing that flies open in the middle of a pantomime and up from the depths comes the demon king with a flash of lightning and a puff of smoke. When he's said his piece, the demon king disappears by the same route.

Well, 'Mephistopheles' said to the old stage manager, 'Does that trap door still work?' I'd love to make my first entrance that way and then go down again at the end of the opera!'

'Well now, sorry, that trap door hasn't been used for years and years and years. . . But I tell you what I'll do. I'll grease it up a bit and I'll put in some new ropes and it'll be great!' replied the stage manager.

He was as good as his word. What's more, he found a smoke box, a flash box and an old piece of metal sheeting to rattle for a clap of thunder.

On the first night, the audience were startled and delighted by this *coup de théâtre*. Everything worked like a charm. However, at the end of the opera when the heroine Marguerite ascends to heaven and

Mephistopheles is turned aside by an angel, things started to go wrong.

Mephistopheles was standing on the trap all right and he tapped his foot to cue the trap operator below. Immediately, he started to disappear into the nether regions. Unfortunately, though, the lift stuck halfway – leaving the poor old devil visible from the waist up, desperately trying little jumps to get it going again!

At that moment, there was a joyful shout from the gallery: 'Hurrah, boys, hell's full!'

# Keith Waterhouse

C.B.E.

Writer, Playwright

The new young sports reporter on the *Clogthorpe Mercury* was satisfactory in all respects but one. Finally, towards the end of his first football season, the editor thought he'd better have a word.

'Look, son, your soccer reporting is brilliant. It is up there with the best. But it has one flaw. Every week, you start your football story in exactly the same way – or nearly the same way. You either write, 'At a home match on Saturday, Clogthorpe beat the visitors three-nil,' or, 'At an away match on Saturday, Clogthorpe lost to Scumborough two-four.' Can't you vary it a bit, lad? See if you can give us something a bit different.'

The young reporter saw at once where he had been going wrong, and agreed to think about it.

The following week he turned in a report which began as follows:

> 'There are three cardinal virtues – faith, hope and charity. Of these, most of us would agree with St. Paul that charity is the chief among them. At a charity match on Saturday, Clogthorpe beat the visitors. . .'

# Katharine Whitehorn
Columnist, Author and Broadcaster

Machiavelli was asked on his deathbed to renounce the Devil. He refused, with the words: 'This is no time to be making enemies.'

*　　*　　*

A ship is going full steam ahead through thick mists. It sends out a signal to another ship, which it sights in its radarscope: 'Turn 20 degrees to port.'

It receives the signal: 'No. You turn 20 degrees to starboard.'

The first repeats: 'Turn 20 degrees to port; I am a supertanker.'

And receives: 'Turn 20 degrees to starboard; I AM A LIGHTHOUSE.'

*　　*　　*

A man at a party accidentally drops his glass eye into a tray of olives. Another man, who is talking hard, inadvertently eats it.

Some hours later he suffers stomach pains, is rushed to hospital, and investigations take place – including a doctor peering up him with a proctoscope.

The doctor suddenly looks up, affronted, and walks round to the man's head, saying, 'I don't think you trust me!'

# The Rt. Hon. Viscount Whitelaw

K.T., C.H., M.C.

A note that was put on the mantelpiece of a husband, who was always out enjoying himself, read:

> 'The day before yesterday you came home yesterday morning. Yesterday you have come home this morning. If today you come home tomorrow, you will find that I left you yesterday!'

# Kenneth Wolstenholme

D.F.C.

Sports Commentator

A sign in a hotel bedroom read:

> 'In order to ensure a measure of privacy, no
> evening visit will be made by a chambermaid
> unless requested. Should you need service, please
> telephone the Duty Housekeeper, who will be
> most pleased to attend to your requirements.
> Service is available from 6 pm until 10 pm.'

**(N.B. This is a true sign I saw in a hotel!)**

\*  \*  \*

A boy asked his father the meaning of the words
'irritation, aggravation and frustration'.

The father replied: 'If the telephone rings and a voice
asks, "Is Mike there?" and you reply that there is no one
there called Mike and you suggest he has the wrong
number, which he denies – that is irritation. If the
telephone rings a few minutes later and the same man
asks, "Is Mike there?" and you again reply, rather
heatedly, that there is no one there called Mike and the
caller must have the wrong number – that's aggravation.
If, some minutes later, the telephone rings again and a
voice says, "This is Mike here. Are there any messages?"
– that's frustration!'

# Other Titles from Piatkus Books

If you have enjoyed *Cheers!* you may be interested in other books published by Piatkus for after-dinner speakers and communicators. Titles include:

**100 Best After-Dinner Stories from the Famous** Phyllis Shindler
**100 Favourite After-Dinner Stories from the Famous** Phyllis Shindler
**Confident Conversation: How to talk in any business or social situation** Dr Lillian Glass
**Confident Speaking: How to communicate effectively using the Power Talk System** Christian H Godefroy and Stephanie Barrat
**It Gives Me Great Pleasure: The complete after-dinner speaker's handbook** Herbert Prochnow
**My Lords, Ladies and Gentlemen: The best and funniest after-dinner stories from the Famous** Phyllis Shindler
**Powerspeak: The complete guide to public speaking and presentation** Dorothy Leeds
**Raise Your Glasses: The best and wittiest anecdotes and after-dinner stories from the Famous** Phyllis Shindler

For a free brochure with further information on our range of titles, please write to:

Piatkus Books
Freepost 7 (WD 4505)
London W1E 4EZ

PIATKUS

**ALBANY APARTMENTS**
**OBAN**


**BARAVULLIN COTTAGE**
**LEDAIG**
**Nr. BENDERLOCH**

# Cheers!

Entertaining
After-Dinner Stories
from the Famous

ALBANY APARTMENTS
OBAN

BARAVULLIN COTTAGE
LEDAIG
Nr. BENDERLOCH

**Other books by Phyllis Shindler, also published by Piatkus:**

*My Lords, Ladies and Gentlemen*
*100 Best After-Dinner Stories*
*100 Favourite After-Dinner Stories from The Famous*
*Raise Your Glasses*